EMMANUEL JOSEPH

Crypto for Crisis, Revolutionizing Global Military and Health Aid with Blockchain

Copyright © 2025 by Emmanuel Joseph

All rights reserved. No part of this publication may be reproduced, stored or transmitted in any form or by any means, electronic, mechanical, photocopying, recording, scanning, or otherwise without written permission from the publisher. It is illegal to copy this book, post it to a website, or distribute it by any other means without permission.

First edition

This book was professionally typeset on Reedsy.
Find out more at reedsy.com

Contents

1. Chapter 1 — 1
2. Chapter 1: The Genesis of a New Era — 4
3. Chapter 2: The Anatomy of Blockchain — 6
4. Chapter 3: The Crisis Landscape — 8
5. Chapter 4: Blockchain in Military Aid — 10
6. Chapter 5: Blockchain in Health Aid — 12
7. Chapter 6: Case Studies: Blockchain in Action — 14
8. Chapter 7: The Role of Cryptocurrency in Aid — 16
9. Chapter 8: Building the Infrastructure — 18
10. Chapter 9: Ethical Considerations — 20
11. Chapter 10: The Future of Blockchain in Aid — 21
12. Chapter 11: Challenges and Limitations — 23
13. Chapter 12: A Call to Action — 24

Chapter 1

Introduction: A New Frontier in Crisis Response

In an era defined by rapid technological advancement and escalating global challenges, the need for innovative solutions to address crises has never been more urgent. From devastating natural disasters and protracted armed conflicts to unprecedented health emergencies, the world is grappling with a growing number of complex crises that demand swift, efficient, and transparent responses. Traditional systems of delivering military and health aid, while well-intentioned, often fall short due to bureaucratic inefficiencies, corruption, and a lack of coordination among stakeholders. Enter blockchain technology—a groundbreaking innovation that promises to revolutionize the way aid is delivered, tracked, and managed. This book, *Crypto for Crisis: Revolutionizing Global Military and Health Aid with Blockchain*, explores how this transformative technology can address the shortcomings of conventional systems and pave the way for a more equitable and effective approach to crisis response.

Blockchain, at its core, is a decentralized digital ledger that records transactions in a secure, transparent, and immutable manner. Originally developed as the underlying technology for cryptocurrencies like Bitcoin, blockchain has since evolved into a versatile tool with applications across industries, from finance to supply chain management. Its potential to enhance transparency, reduce fraud, and streamline processes makes it uniquely suited to the challenges of global aid delivery. By eliminating the need for intermediaries and providing a tamper-proof record of transactions, blockchain can ensure that resources reach their intended recipients quickly and efficiently, even in the most challenging environments. This book delves into the mechanics of blockchain, its ethical implications, and its practical applications in military and health aid, offering a comprehensive roadmap for its integration into crisis response systems.

The urgency of this discussion cannot be overstated. In recent years, the world has witnessed a series of crises that have exposed the limitations of traditional aid systems. During the COVID-19 pandemic, for instance, the global distribution of medical supplies was plagued by delays, mismanagement, and allegations of corruption. Similarly, in conflict zones, the diversion of military aid to unintended recipients has undermined efforts to stabilize regions and protect vulnerable populations. These failures highlight the need for a paradigm shift in how aid is delivered—one that prioritizes transparency, accountability, and efficiency. Blockchain technology offers a way forward, providing a framework for rebuilding trust in global aid systems and ensuring that resources are used effectively to save lives and alleviate suffering.

However, the adoption of blockchain in crisis response is not without its challenges. Technical barriers, such as the need for reliable internet connectivity and user-friendly interfaces, must be addressed to ensure that the technology is accessible in resource-scarce environments. Ethical considerations, including data privacy and the risk of excluding vulnerable populations, must also be carefully navigated to ensure that blockchain serves as a force for good. This book does not shy away from these complexities; instead, it provides a balanced exploration of both the opportunities and risks associated with blockchain, offering practical solutions and actionable insights for policymakers, aid organizations, and technologists alike.

Ultimately, *Crypto for Crisis* is a call to action—a rallying cry for individuals and organizations to embrace innovation and work together to build a more resilient and equitable world. By harnessing the power of blockchain, we can transform the way military and health aid is delivered, ensuring that help reaches those who need it most, when they need it most. This book is

CHAPTER 1

not just a theoretical exploration of blockchain's potential; it is a practical guide for turning that potential into reality. As we stand at the intersection of technology and humanitarianism, the choices we make today will shape the future of global aid. The time to act is now.

2

Chapter 1: The Genesis of a New Era

In a world increasingly defined by technological innovation, the emergence of blockchain technology has opened doors to unprecedented possibilities. The concept of using cryptocurrency and blockchain for global aid began as a whisper among tech enthusiasts but quickly gained traction as crises around the world exposed the inefficiencies of traditional systems. From natural disasters to pandemics, the need for transparent, secure, and rapid distribution of resources became glaringly apparent. This chapter explores the origins of blockchain technology and how its decentralized nature offers a solution to the bureaucratic bottlenecks that often hinder aid delivery. It sets the stage for understanding how this technology could revolutionize military and health aid.

The idea of using blockchain for humanitarian purposes was first tested in small-scale projects, such as providing aid to refugees in war-torn regions. These early experiments demonstrated the potential for blockchain to ensure that funds and resources reached their intended recipients without being siphoned off by corrupt intermediaries. The success of these pilot programs sparked interest among global organizations, leading to broader discussions about scaling the technology for larger crises. This chapter delves into the initial challenges faced by these projects, including skepticism from traditional aid organizations and the technical hurdles of implementing blockchain in resource-scarce environments.

CHAPTER 1: THE GENESIS OF A NEW ERA

As the world entered an era of heightened geopolitical tensions and frequent health emergencies, the limitations of conventional aid systems became impossible to ignore. Blockchain's ability to provide transparency, traceability, and accountability offered a glimmer of hope. This chapter concludes by introducing the central thesis of the book: that blockchain technology, when applied thoughtfully, can transform the way military and health aid is delivered, ensuring that help arrives faster, reaches further, and is distributed more fairly than ever before.

3

Chapter 2: The Anatomy of Blockchain

To understand how blockchain can revolutionize global aid, it is essential to grasp the fundamentals of the technology itself. Blockchain is a decentralized digital ledger that records transactions across a network of computers. Each transaction is grouped into a "block," which is then linked to the previous block, forming a "chain." This structure ensures that once data is recorded, it cannot be altered without altering all subsequent blocks, making the system highly secure and resistant to fraud. This chapter provides a detailed explanation of how blockchain works, breaking down complex concepts like cryptography, consensus mechanisms, and smart contracts into accessible terms.

The decentralized nature of blockchain eliminates the need for intermediaries, such as banks or government agencies, which often slow down aid distribution. Instead, transactions can be verified and recorded by the network itself, ensuring speed and efficiency. This chapter explores real-world examples of blockchain applications outside of aid, such as supply chain management and financial services, to illustrate its potential. By drawing parallels between these industries and global aid, the chapter demonstrates how blockchain's core features can address the unique challenges of crisis response.

However, blockchain is not without its limitations. This chapter also examines the technical and logistical challenges of implementing blockchain in

CHAPTER 2: THE ANATOMY OF BLOCKCHAIN

crisis zones, including issues like internet connectivity, energy consumption, and the need for user-friendly interfaces. It emphasizes that while blockchain is a powerful tool, its success depends on thoughtful design and adaptation to the specific needs of aid delivery. The chapter concludes by highlighting the importance of collaboration between technologists, aid organizations, and policymakers to unlock blockchain's full potential.

4

Chapter 3: The Crisis Landscape

The world is no stranger to crises, but the 21st century has seen an alarming increase in both their frequency and complexity. From armed conflicts and natural disasters to pandemics and climate change, the demand for effective aid delivery has never been greater. This chapter provides an overview of the current crisis landscape, examining the types of emergencies that require military and health aid and the common challenges faced by responders. It highlights the inefficiencies of traditional aid systems, such as delays in funding, lack of transparency, and the diversion of resources by corrupt actors.

One of the most significant challenges in crisis response is the coordination of multiple stakeholders, including governments, non-governmental organizations (NGOs), and private sector partners. This chapter explores how blockchain can streamline this process by creating a shared, immutable record of transactions and actions. For example, during a natural disaster, blockchain could be used to track the distribution of supplies, ensuring that every item reaches its intended destination. Similarly, in a health crisis, blockchain could facilitate the rapid deployment of medical resources and the secure sharing of patient data.

The chapter also addresses the ethical considerations of using blockchain in crisis response. While the technology offers many benefits, it also raises questions about data privacy, surveillance, and the potential exclusion of vulnerable populations who lack access to digital tools. By examining these issues, the chapter underscores the need for a balanced approach that leverages blockchain's strengths while mitigating its risks. It concludes by arguing that blockchain is not a panacea but a valuable tool that, when used responsibly, can significantly enhance the effectiveness of global aid.

5

Chapter 4: Blockchain in Military Aid

Military aid plays a critical role in responding to conflicts and stabilizing regions in crisis. However, the delivery of military aid is often fraught with challenges, including corruption, mismanagement, and the diversion of resources to unintended recipients. This chapter explores how blockchain can address these issues by providing a transparent and tamper-proof record of aid transactions. For example, blockchain could be used to track the shipment of weapons, ensuring that they reach legitimate recipients and are not sold on the black market.

The chapter also examines the potential for blockchain to enhance coordination among military and humanitarian actors. In complex conflict zones, multiple organizations often operate independently, leading to duplication of efforts and gaps in coverage. Blockchain could serve as a shared platform for these organizations to coordinate their activities, share information, and allocate resources more efficiently. This would not only improve the effectiveness of military aid but also reduce the risk of unintended consequences, such as civilian casualties.

However, the use of blockchain in military aid also raises ethical and security concerns. This chapter discusses the potential risks, such as the exposure of sensitive information to adversaries and the use of blockchain for surveillance purposes. It emphasizes the need for robust safeguards to protect the integrity of the system and the privacy of its users. The chapter concludes by arguing that, despite these challenges, blockchain has the potential to transform military aid into a more transparent, accountable, and effective tool for promoting global stability.

6

Chapter 5: Blockchain in Health Aid

Health crises, whether caused by pandemics, natural disasters, or conflicts, demand rapid and efficient responses. Yet, traditional health aid systems are often hindered by bureaucratic red tape, lack of transparency, and the misallocation of resources. This chapter explores how blockchain can revolutionize health aid by enabling the secure and efficient distribution of medical supplies, tracking the movement of vaccines, and ensuring the integrity of health data. For example, during a pandemic, blockchain could be used to verify the authenticity of vaccines and track their distribution to prevent counterfeiting.

The chapter also highlights the potential for blockchain to improve the management of health data in crisis zones. In many cases, health records are fragmented or inaccessible, making it difficult to provide effective care. Blockchain could serve as a decentralized platform for storing and sharing health data, ensuring that patients receive the care they need regardless of where they are. This would be particularly valuable in refugee camps or conflict zones, where populations are often displaced and lack access to traditional healthcare systems.

However, the use of blockchain in health aid also raises important ethical questions, particularly regarding data privacy and consent. This chapter discusses the need for clear guidelines and regulations to ensure that health data is used responsibly and that patients' rights are protected. It concludes

CHAPTER 5: BLOCKCHAIN IN HEALTH AID

by arguing that, with the right safeguards in place, blockchain can play a transformative role in improving the delivery of health aid and saving lives in times of crisis.

7

Chapter 6: Case Studies: Blockchain in Action

This chapter presents real-world examples of blockchain being used to deliver military and health aid. It begins with a case study of a pilot project in a conflict zone, where blockchain was used to track the distribution of food and medical supplies to refugees. The project demonstrated how blockchain could reduce corruption and ensure that aid reached its intended recipients. The chapter also examines a health crisis response in which blockchain was used to manage the distribution of vaccines during a pandemic, highlighting the technology's ability to prevent counterfeiting and ensure transparency.

Another case study focuses on the use of blockchain in coordinating international military aid during a natural disaster. The project involved multiple countries and organizations working together to deliver supplies and personnel to the affected region. Blockchain served as a shared platform for tracking resources and coordinating efforts, resulting in a more efficient and effective response. The chapter also explores a project in which blockchain was used to provide financial aid to disaster victims, enabling them to receive funds directly through cryptocurrency wallets.

These case studies illustrate the potential of blockchain to transform aid delivery, but they also reveal the challenges and limitations of the technology.

CHAPTER 6: CASE STUDIES: BLOCKCHAIN IN ACTION

The chapter concludes by emphasizing the importance of learning from these experiences to refine and improve blockchain-based solutions for future crises.

8

Chapter 7: The Role of Cryptocurrency in Aid

Cryptocurrency, as a digital asset built on blockchain technology, offers unique advantages for global aid. This chapter explores how cryptocurrency can be used to facilitate rapid and secure transactions, bypassing traditional financial systems that may be slow or inaccessible in crisis zones. For example, during a natural disaster, cryptocurrency could be used to provide immediate financial assistance to victims, enabling them to purchase essential supplies without waiting for banks to reopen.

The chapter also examines the potential for cryptocurrency to reduce transaction costs and increase the efficiency of aid delivery. Traditional financial systems often involve high fees and lengthy processing times, which can delay the distribution of resources. Cryptocurrency, on the other hand, allows for near-instantaneous transactions at a fraction of the cost. This could be particularly valuable in situations where time is of the essence, such as during a health crisis or military conflict.

However, the use of cryptocurrency in aid also raises concerns about volatility, regulation, and accessibility. This chapter discusses these challenges and explores potential solutions, such as the use of stablecoins (cryptocurrencies pegged to stable assets like the US dollar) and the development of user-friendly platforms for managing digital assets. It concludes by arguing that, despite these challenges, cryptocurrency has the potential to play a significant role in revolutionizing global aid.

9

Chapter 8: Building the Infrastructure

For blockchain to be effectively used in global aid, the necessary infrastructure must be in place. This chapter explores the technical, logistical, and regulatory requirements for implementing blockchain in crisis zones. It begins by discussing the need for reliable internet connectivity, which is often lacking in remote or conflict-affected areas. The chapter examines potential solutions, such as satellite-based internet and mesh networks, that could provide the connectivity needed to support blockchain applications.

The chapter also addresses the importance of developing user-friendly interfaces and tools that enable aid workers and recipients to interact with blockchain systems. Many people in crisis zones may lack the technical expertise to use blockchain directly, so it is essential to create intuitive platforms that simplify the process. The chapter explores examples of such platforms and discusses the role of training and education in ensuring their successful adoption.

Finally, the chapter examines the regulatory landscape for blockchain and cryptocurrency in the context of global aid. It highlights the need for clear and consistent regulations that support innovation while protecting against fraud and abuse. The chapter concludes by emphasizing the importance of collaboration between governments, international organizations, and the private sector to build the infrastructure needed to make blockchain a viable

CHAPTER 8: BUILDING THE INFRASTRUCTURE

tool for crisis response.

10

Chapter 9: Ethical Considerations

The use of blockchain in global aid raises important ethical questions that must be addressed to ensure that the technology is used responsibly. This chapter explores issues such as data privacy, surveillance, and the potential exclusion of vulnerable populations. It begins by discussing the importance of protecting the privacy of aid recipients, particularly in conflict zones or authoritarian regimes where sensitive information could be used against them.

The chapter also examines the potential for blockchain to be used as a tool for surveillance, either by governments or other actors. While blockchain's transparency can enhance accountability, it also raises concerns about the misuse of data. The chapter explores potential safeguards, such as encryption and anonymization, that could protect against these risks.

Finally, the chapter addresses the risk of excluding vulnerable populations who lack access to digital tools or the internet. It emphasizes the need for inclusive design and the provision of alternative options for those who cannot use blockchain directly. The chapter concludes by arguing that, while blockchain offers many benefits, its ethical implications must be carefully considered to ensure that it serves the needs of all people, particularly those in crisis.

11

Chapter 10: The Future of Blockchain in Aid

As blockchain technology continues to evolve, its potential to revolutionize global aid is likely to grow. This chapter explores emerging trends and innovations that could further enhance the effectiveness of blockchain in crisis response. It begins by discussing the development of more advanced smart contracts, which could automate complex aid delivery processes and reduce the need for intermediaries.

The chapter also examines the potential for blockchain to integrate with other emerging technologies, such as artificial intelligence (AI) and the Internet of Things (IoT). For example, AI could be used to analyze blockchain data and identify patterns or trends that could inform aid strategies. IoT devices, such as sensors and drones, could provide real-time data that is recorded on the blockchain, enabling more accurate and timely responses to crises.

Finally, the chapter explores the potential for blockchain to empower local communities and enable them to take a more active role in crisis response. By providing a transparent and decentralized platform for managing resources, blockchain could help communities build resilience and reduce their dependence on external aid. The chapter concludes by envisioning a future in which blockchain is an integral part of global aid, enabling faster, fairer, and more effective responses to crises around the world.

12

Chapter 11: Challenges and Limitations

While blockchain holds great promise for revolutionizing global aid, it is not without its challenges and limitations. This chapter explores the technical, logistical, and social barriers that must be overcome to realize its full potential. It begins by discussing the issue of scalability, as blockchain networks can become slow and inefficient as they grow in size. The chapter examines potential solutions, such as layer-two protocols and sharding, that could improve scalability without compromising security.

The chapter also addresses the challenge of energy consumption, as blockchain networks often require significant amounts of electricity to operate. This is particularly problematic in crisis zones, where energy resources may be scarce. The chapter explores alternative consensus mechanisms, such as proof-of-stake, that could reduce the environmental impact of blockchain.

Finally, the chapter examines the social and cultural barriers to adopting blockchain in global aid. Many aid organizations and governments may be resistant to change, particularly if they are unfamiliar with the technology. The chapter emphasizes the need for education and advocacy to build trust and encourage the adoption of blockchain. It concludes by arguing that, while these challenges are significant, they are not insurmountable, and with the right approach, blockchain can become a powerful tool for crisis response.

13

Chapter 12: A Call to Action

The final chapter of the book serves as a call to action, urging readers to recognize the potential of blockchain to transform global aid and to take steps to support its adoption. It begins by summarizing the key arguments presented in the book, emphasizing the need for transparency, efficiency, and accountability in crisis response. The chapter highlights the role that blockchain can play in achieving these goals, while also acknowledging the challenges and limitations that must be addressed.

The chapter then outlines specific actions that readers can take to support the use of blockchain in global aid. This includes advocating for policy changes, supporting pilot projects, and contributing to the development of blockchain infrastructure. The chapter also emphasizes the importance of collaboration, urging governments, NGOs, and the private sector to work together to harness the power of blockchain for the greater good.

Finally, the chapter concludes with a vision of a future in which blockchain is widely used to deliver military and health aid, ensuring that help reaches those who need it most. It calls on readers to embrace this vision and to take action to make it a reality, reminding them that the success of blockchain in global aid depends on the collective efforts of individuals and organizations around the world.

Book Description: Crypto for Crisis: Revolutionizing Global Military and Health Aid with Blockchain

CHAPTER 12: A CALL TO ACTION

In a world increasingly defined by uncertainty and upheaval, the need for effective and transparent systems to deliver aid during crises has never been more critical. *Crypto for Crisis: Revolutionizing Global Military and Health Aid with Blockchain* is a groundbreaking exploration of how blockchain technology can transform the way we respond to global emergencies. From natural disasters and armed conflicts to pandemics and climate-related crises, this book delves into the challenges of traditional aid systems and presents blockchain as a powerful solution to overcome inefficiencies, corruption, and delays.

At its heart, this book is a journey into the potential of blockchain to create a more equitable and accountable world. It begins by unraveling the complexities of blockchain technology, breaking down its core principles—such as decentralization, transparency, and immutability—into accessible terms. Readers will discover how these features can address the persistent issues plaguing military and health aid, from the mismanagement of resources to the lack of coordination among stakeholders. Through real-world examples and case studies, the book illustrates how blockchain has already been successfully deployed in pilot projects, offering a glimpse of what's possible when innovation meets humanitarian need.

But *Crypto for Crisis* is not just a celebration of technology; it is a thoughtful examination of the challenges and ethical considerations that come with its adoption. The book tackles critical questions about data privacy, accessibility, and the risk of excluding vulnerable populations who may lack access to digital tools. It also explores the technical and logistical hurdles of implementing blockchain in crisis zones, such as the need for reliable internet connectivity and user-friendly interfaces. By addressing these challenges head-on, the book provides a balanced and realistic perspective on how blockchain can be integrated into global aid systems responsibly and effectively.

What sets this book apart is its actionable vision for the future. It goes beyond theory to offer practical steps for policymakers, aid organizations, and technologists to harness the power of blockchain in crisis response. From building the necessary infrastructure to fostering collaboration among diverse stakeholders, the book outlines a roadmap for turning blockchain's potential into reality. It also highlights emerging trends, such as the integration of blockchain with artificial intelligence and the Internet of Things, that could further enhance its impact in the years to come.

Ultimately, *Crypto for Crisis* is a call to action—a compelling argument for embracing innovation to create a more resilient and compassionate world. It challenges readers to rethink the status quo and imagine a future where aid is delivered faster, more transparently, and more equitably than ever before. Whether you're a technologist, a humanitarian worker, or simply someone who cares about making a difference, this book will inspire you to join the movement to revolutionize global aid. The time to act is now, and blockchain is the tool that can help us build a brighter future for all.

www.ingramcontent.com/pod-product-compliance
Lightning Source LLC
LaVergne TN
LVHW020741090526
838202LV00057BA/6170